BERKLEE PRESS

8 ESSENTIALS OF DRUMMING

GROOVES,
FUNDAMENTALS,
AND
MUSICIANSHIP

By Ron Savage

Edited by
Jonathan Feist and
Susan Gedutis Lindsay

D0584823

Berklee Press

Vice President: David Kusek
Dean of Continuing Education: Debbie Cavalier
Managing Editor: Jonathan Feist
Editorial Assistants: Emily Goldstein, Rajasri Millikarjuna, Meredith White
Director of Business Affairs: Robert F. Green
Senior Designer: Robert Heath

ISBN 978-0-87639-051-1

DISTRIBUTED BY

1140 Boylston Street
Boston, MA 02215-3693 USA
(617) 747-2146

Visit Berklee Press Online at
www.berkleepress.com

HAL•LEONARD®
CORPORATION
7777 W. BLUEMOUND RD. P.O. BOX 13819
MILWAUKEE, WISCONSIN 53213

Visit Hal Leonard Online at
www.halleonard.com

Copyright © 2009 Berklee Press
All Rights Reserved

No part of this publication may be reproduced in any form or by
any means without the prior written permission of the Publisher.

Contents

CD Tracks

Track 1.   Four on the Floor, Full Band
Track 2.   Four on the Floor, No Drums
Track 3.   Four-on-the-Floor Variation, Full Band
Track 4.   Four-on-the-Floor Variation, No Drums
Track 5.   Funky Sixteenth, Full Band
Track 6.   Funky Sixteenth, No Drums
Track 7.   Drums-a-Go-Go, Full Band
Track 8.   Drums-a-Go-Go, No Drums
Track 9.   The Shuffle, Full Band
Track 10.   The Shuffle, No Drums
Track 11.   The Motown, Full Band
Track 12.   The Motown, No Drums
Track 13.   The 12/8 Shuffle, Full Band
Track 14.   The 12/8 Shuffle, No Drums
Track 15.   Shuffle Variation 1. Pop Shuffle, Full Band
Track 16.   Shuffle Variation 1. Pop Shuffle, No Drums
Track 17.   Shuffle Variation 2. Chicago Blues Shuffle, Full Band
Track 18.   Shuffle Variation 2. Chicago Blues Shuffle, No Drums
Track 19.   Standard Pop Ballad, Full Band
Track 20.   Standard Pop Ballad, No Drums
Track 21.   Sixteenth-Note Feel, Full Band
Track 22.   Sixteenth-Note Feel, No Drums
Track 23.   6/8 Slow Jam, Full Band
Track 24.   6/8 Slow Jam, No Drums
Track 25.   Bossa Variation 1, Full Band
Track 26.   Bossa Variation 1, No Drums
Track 27.   Bossa Variation 2, Full Band
Track 28.   Bossa Variation 2, No Drums
Track 29.   Reggae, Full Band
Track 30.   Reggae, No Drums
Track 31.   Calypso, Full Band
Track 32.   Calypso, No Drums
Track 33.   Mambo, Full Band
Track 34.   Mambo, No Drums
Track 35.   Cha-cha, Full Band
Track 36.   Cha-cha, No Drums
Track 37.   Swing, Full Band
Track 38.   Swing, No Drums
Track 39.   Swing Variation 1: Organ Groove, Full Band
Track 40.   Swing Variation 1: Organ Groove, No Drums
Track 41.   Swing Variation 2: Swing in 3/4 Time, Full Band
Track 42.   Swing Variation 2: Swing in 3/4 Time, No Drums
Track 43.   Circles on Snare with Bass Drum, Full Band
Track 44.   Circles on Snare with Bass Drum, No Drums
Track 45.   Right-hand Brush Pattern for 4/4 Jazz
Track 46.   Left-hand Brush Pattern for 4/4 Jazz
Track 47.   4/4 Jazz with Brushes, Both Hands, Full Band
Track 48.   4/4 Jazz with Brushes, Both Hands, No Drums
Track 49.   "Suelo's Tune," Full Band
Track 50.   "Suelo's Tune," No Drums

Acknowledgments

Thanks to God, my beautiful wife Lois, my son Xavier, and my daughter Andrea.

Thanks to my parents, who have always believed in me, and all those who cared enough to lend a hand along the way.

Introduction

As the Chair of Berklee's Ensemble Department, I am keenly aware of the challenges drummers face as they prepare for the professional ranks, and it seems to get more challenging all the time. As technology quickly erodes musical boundaries, any serious drummer must have a diversity of skills.

That said, the essentials taught in this text are some of the *fundamental* skills that I feel are necessary for the contemporary drummer. Many of the concepts and examples in this book are taken directly from the Berklee curriculum and closely mirror the expectations that we have for our graduating drummers.

These examples will come to life only when you put them into a musical context. Listen to recordings of your favorite drummers to get ideas for interpretation and application. Then find some musical friends, and jam!

Drum-Set Notation Key

	Bass Drum	Snare Drum	Cross Stick	Rim Shot	Hi Tom	Mid Tom	Floor Tom	Hi-Hat w/ Stick	Ride Cymbal	Hi-Hat w/ Foot	Ride Bell
Abbr.	B.D.	S.D.	C.S.	R.S.	H.T.	M.T.	F.T.	H.H.	Ride	HHw/Foot	Ride

CHAPTER 1. Ergonomics: The Body Is the Beat

Think about a great—perhaps even awe-inspiring—drum performance you have witnessed. Recall the ease with which the drummer seemed to play, the relaxed attitude, and the excellence displayed in the drummer's ability to meet the demands of the music. These attributes all start with our posture and grip—the way we sit and move, and the way we hold and control the sticks.

Posture

Because each person's body design is different, it is important to base our movements on our own bodies, rather than some predetermined notion of what our posture should look like. A person with longer legs will sit higher than a shorter person to allow for the relaxed extension of the limbs. A person with shorter arms will set up the drums in a way that will allow them to easily reach every part of the drum kit.

In general, sit with your back straight and your arms straight and relaxed, hanging naturally and pointing toward the floor. Then raise your forearms so that your elbows are bent at a 90-degree angle, keeping your shoulders and arms as relaxed as possible. Keep your back straight. This is your natural playing position.

With the correct seat height, the drummer's legs and lower body are relaxed and balanced.

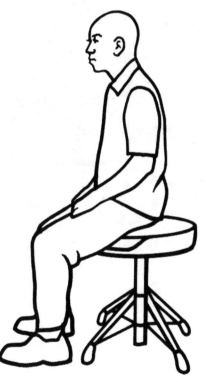

Fig. 1.1. Correct seat height

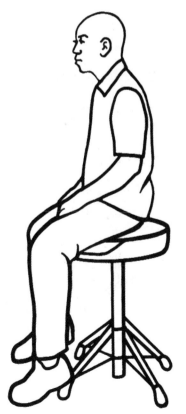

With the seat too high, legs can become overextended, making it difficult to maintain balance.

Fig. 1.2. Seat too high

With the seat too low, leg muscles are restricted and tire easily.

Fig. 1.3. Seat too low

Notice how the entire drum set is set up to allow for an easy reach to all cymbals and drums.

Fig. 1.4. Drummer properly positioned at drum set

Grip

Hold your sticks at the *fulcrum*, about a third up from the butt end. Rest your other fingers loosely on the stick without applying any pressure. This is known as a *matched grip*—the most common way to hold the sticks.

Fig. 1.5. Grip

CHAPTER 2. Pop, Rock, and R&B

The syncopated rhythms and pumped-up drumbeats of today's pop, rock, and r&b have common roots that reach back to the early 1900s and the origins of American popular music.

The funky rhythms of the New Orleans parade bands gave birth to blues and gospel in the African American south. As this music spread to the Midwest—especially Chicago—and Texas and the Southeast in the 1930s, jazz and blues inspired a style of dance music termed "r&b."

Since the 1950s, rock and pop have dominated musical culture. In the 1960s and 1970s, the growth of Motown soul and the funkiness of James Brown combined with rock 'n' roll to complete the foundation that today's hip-hop is built upon.

LISTENING

Essential listening to gain a deeper understanding of the grooves in this chapter should include Motown artists, Louis Jordan, Big Mama Thornton, Chuck Berry, James Brown, Cream, the Beatles, Jimi Hendrix, the Rolling Stones, Aretha Franklin, Michael Jackson, Led Zeppelin, and Parliament Funkadelic.

Four on the Floor

This beat is commonly used in all contemporary music: hip-hop, rock, pop, rap, country. Its strength lies in its simplicity and its clarity.

TRACK 1,
TRACK 2

Four-on-the-Floor Variation

Opening the hi-hat on the offbeat creates the "house" music effect. Allowing the hi-hat to ring open on every other note creates a heavier pop/rock feel.

TRACK 3,
TRACK 4

PRACTICE TIP

Practice slowly to feel each part.

Funky Sixteenth

This medium-tempo groove displays a common interpretation of a sixteenth-note groove, based on a sixteenth-note hi-hat feel.

TRACK 5,
TRACK 6

Drums-a-Go-Go

Today's hip-hop drummers play the beat with a slight "swing," an approach that derived from the "go-go" and "new jack" beats of the 1990s.

TRACK 7,
TRACK 8

CHAPTER 3. The Shuffle

The shuffle is the most universal drumbeat. It is found in pop, rock, jazz, blues, country, gospel, and r&b. It may be the most common feel, yet it is also the most deceptively complex. It may not take long to get control of the coordination, but developing a consistent, deep groove can take some time.

LISTENING

Art Blakey, Shadow Wilson, Bernard "Pretty" Purdie, and various Motown artists.

The Shuffle

Big band jazz drummers of the 1930s and 1940s originated and popularized this shuffle, which later became a mainstay of pop drumming through the music of the Motown era in the 1960s and 1970s. Always play it with a strong triplet feel.

TRACK 9,
TRACK 10

PRACTICE TIP

Always start slow with a metronome. Hands should be at equal volume with slight accents on beats 2 and 4.

The Motown

TRACK 11,
TRACK 12

($\downarrow$) = ghost note played softly

The 12/8 Shuffle

Although all shuffles have a triplet feel, in this shuffle you actually play all the triplets on the hi-hat or ride.

TRACK 13,
TRACK 14

Slightly varying the ride or bass drum pattern can offer many possibilities. Here are two variations:

Shuffle Variation 1. Pop Shuffle

TRACK 15,
TRACK 16

Shuffle Variation 2. Chicago Blues Shuffle

TRACK 17,
TRACK 18

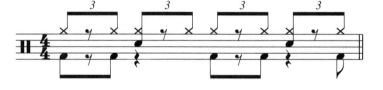

CHAPTER 4. Slow Grooves

Maintaining a deep groove at very slow tempos can be one of the most challenging tasks drummers face. It is something most drummers rarely focus on until they need it—and sometimes, that's too late. Maintaining a slow and steady groove is not as easy as it would appear.

LISTENING

Pop and r&b love songs, blues, and gospel recordings.

Standard Pop Ballad

This groove is found often in pop, rock, gospel, and r&b.

TRACK 19,
TRACK 20

PRACTICE TIP

Challenge yourself by practicing all slow grooves at 40 bpm on the metronome. It will help give you a sense of controlling the space between notes.

Sixteenth-Note Feel

Remember to relax your body. Usually, the more notes we play, the more we tend to tense up.

TRACK 21,
TRACK 22

6/8 Slow Jam

This groove hearkens back to its blues and gospel origins. Play with attitude.

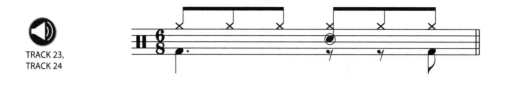

TRACK 23,
TRACK 24

On slower tempos, the sound of the rim click on this snare drum is often substituted for the snare sound.

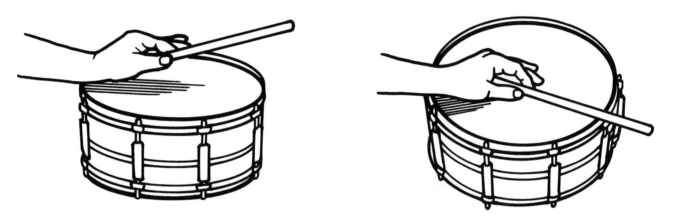

Fig. 4.1. Rim-click positioning

PRACTICE TIP

Practice getting a solid "knock" sound with the rim click.

CHAPTER 5. The African Influence: Afro-Cuban, Caribbean, and South American Grooves

A knowledge of the Latin influence is a must for every serious drummer, as many popular styles borrow from the Latin feel. The Latin influence on mid-twentieth-century jazz and r&b musicians led to the creation of funk and rock styles. These Latin influences have deep roots in African drumming.

LISTENING

Jobim, Tito Puente, Horacio "Negro" Hernandez.

Bossa Nova

Born in 1950s Brazil, the term bossa nova means "new beat." It is commonly used in bossa and samba music settings, but on occasion, it may also be heard in pop, rock, and smooth-jazz settings.

PRACTICE TIP

Practice light and relaxed with a slight swing feel.

Bossa Variation 1

TRACK 25,
TRACK 26

Bossa Variation 2

TRACK 27,
TRACK 28

Reggae

Born of 1950s Jamaican protest music and love songs, reggae music has since become a world-wide phenomenon. This groove is typical of the "one drop" style and can be used at a variety of tempos.

LISTENING

Bob Marley.

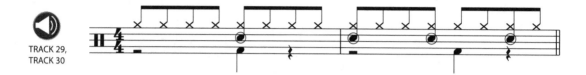

TRACK 29,
TRACK 30

PRACTICE TIP

Play with a swing feel. Notice the rim-click pattern; it is similar to the bossa nova.

Calypso

Originally from the West Indies, Calypso came to popularity with the tropical sounds of steel drum bands. Today, its influence stretches deep into rap and hip-hop.

LISTENING

Soca, steel pan, and dance-hall artists.

TRACK 31,
TRACK 32

Mambo

Introduced to American culture from Cuba through the cha-cha and mambo craze of the 1940s and 1950s, the mambo feel was infused into rock and r&b by Louis Jordan, Ray Charles, and various Motown artists. This instantly recognizable style is often used in jazz and world music settings. Here, it is presented in its original **"American"** interpretation. This version was popularized by jazz greats Max Roach and Art Blakey.

TRACK 33,
TRACK 34

Cha-cha

TRACK 35,
TRACK 36

CHAPTER 6. The 4/4 and 3/4 Jazz Swing Beat

The original drum-set beat, 4/4 jazz defined the way drummers develop four-way coordination. The influence of the swing triplet feel in drumming reaches into all contemporary areas of funk, rock, r&b, and hip-hop.

LISTENING

Art Blakey, Kenny Clarke, and Papa Jo Jones.

Swing

PRACTICE TIP

Play the ride cymbal with a smooth, even touch, with the bass drum very light underneath.

TRACK 37,
TRACK 38

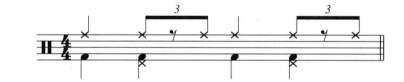

Swing Variation. Organ Groove

TRACK 39,
TRACK 40

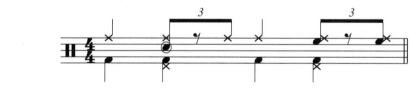

Swing in 3/4 Time

TRACK 41,
TRACK 42

PRACTICE TIP

Remember to keep the bass drum soft.

Using Brushes

Once only an integral part of jazz drummers' vocabularies, brush playing can now be heard frequently in ambient rock, country, world music, smooth jazz, and r&b settings.

LISTENING

Philly Joe Jones, Ed Thigpen, and Vernell Fournier.

PRACTICE TIP

For convenience, in this chapter, we will relate positions on the snare drum head to the face of a clock.

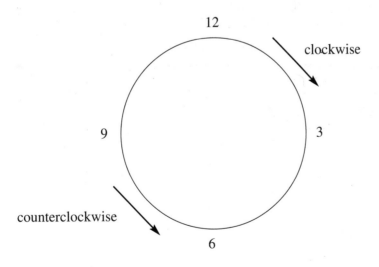

Fig. 6.1. Locations on the drumhead may be compared to a clock face.

Circles for Timekeeping

To learn brush playing, begin by practicing with circles on the drumhead. This timekeeping exercise should give a sense of controlling the sound and touch of the brush on the drumhead.

Set your metronome at 100 bpm. Starting at 12:00, with the right hand, move one complete circle clockwise for every two clicks. Counting "1 and 2 and 3 and 4 and" with the metronome, the brush should pass 6:00 and 12:00 alternately on each click.

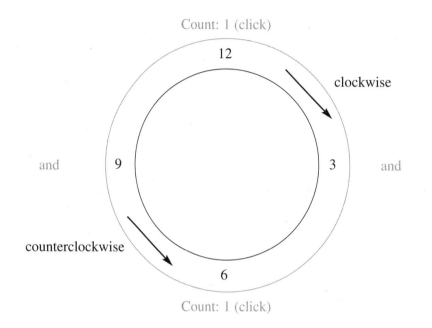

Fig. 6.2. Circles on the drum set

Next, try the same thing moving counterclockwise. After the right hand begins to feel more comfortable, repeat the process with the left hand.

Once you have mastered each hand individually, try moving both hands at the same time. Hands should still reach 12:00 on the number for each count. For each count, hands should move in opposite directions.

Brush Variation 1

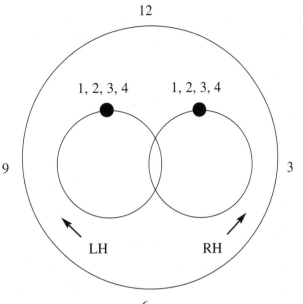

Fig. 6.3. Brush Variation 1

Brush Variation 2

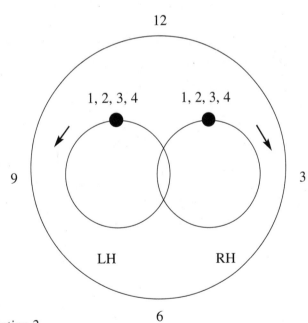

Fig. 6.4. Brush Variation 2

Try different tempos. Begin at a very slow tempo and gradually speed up. Never go faster than a tempo that allows you to stay comfortable and relaxed.

After you gain control over circles, you can begin to use brushes in establishing grooves.

Circles on Snare with Bass Drum

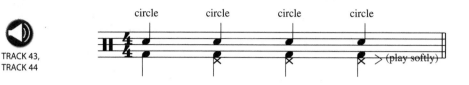

Jazz Swing with Brushes

Jazz swing with brushes requires two hands. The left moves in a sweeping circular motion, and the right strikes the drumhead with the brush tip. Learn each part separately first, then put them together.

Begin by practicing jazz swing pattern with the tip of the brush on the snare drum, with your right hand. Practice this pattern until you can play strokes evenly with the tip of the brush.

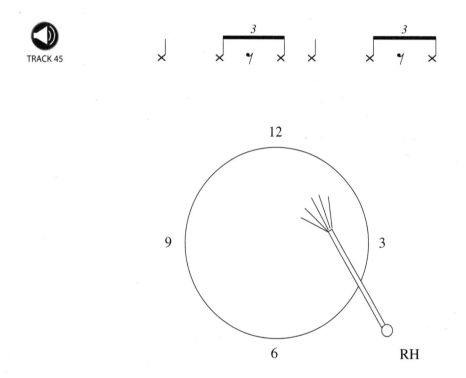

Fig. 6.5. Right-Hand Brush Pattern for 4/4 Jazz

Next, practice sweeping the left hand across the snare on beats 2 and 4.

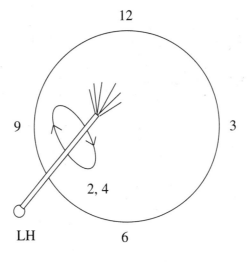

Fig. 6.6. Left-Hand Brush Pattern for 4/4 Jazz

Practice slowly and smoothly with the metronome.

PRACTICE TIP

The brush handle should stay approximately 2 inches off the drum.

Finally, let's put it all together with the bass drum and hi-hat.

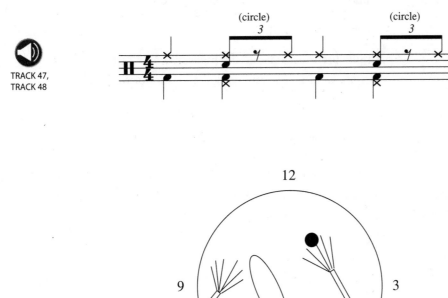

TRACK 47,
TRACK 48

Fig. 6.7. 4/4 Jazz with Brushes, Both Hands

CHAPTER 7. Musicianship Skills: Music and Notation

If you can read or follow a written arrangement, you will be able to function better in a variety of musical settings. This versatility can open doors to a more fulfilling career with many new and rewarding musical experiences.

First, some common musical terms:

Chart   written arrangement

Head   main melody or theme

 **Measures**, also known as bars, are groups of beats.

 **Time signatures** tell us actually how to count the music we are playing. For example, 4/4 tells us we will count "1, 2, 3, 4" for each measure. 3/4 tells us we will count "1, 2, 3" for each measure. 6/8 tells us we will count "1, 2, 3, 4, 5, 6" for each measure.

 Single barlines separate the measures. Each time we get to a barline, we are beginning a new measure or bar.

 Double barlines separate segments of a song.

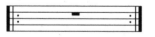 **Slashes** tell us when we should be playing the beat during the song.

 **Repeat signs** indicate which segments of the music should be played a second time (repeated).

 Rehearsal letters or numbers give us common reference starting points when rehearsing.

Dynamics tell us what volume to play.

p	*piano*, play softly
mf	*mezzo-forte*, play medium
f	*forte*, play loudly
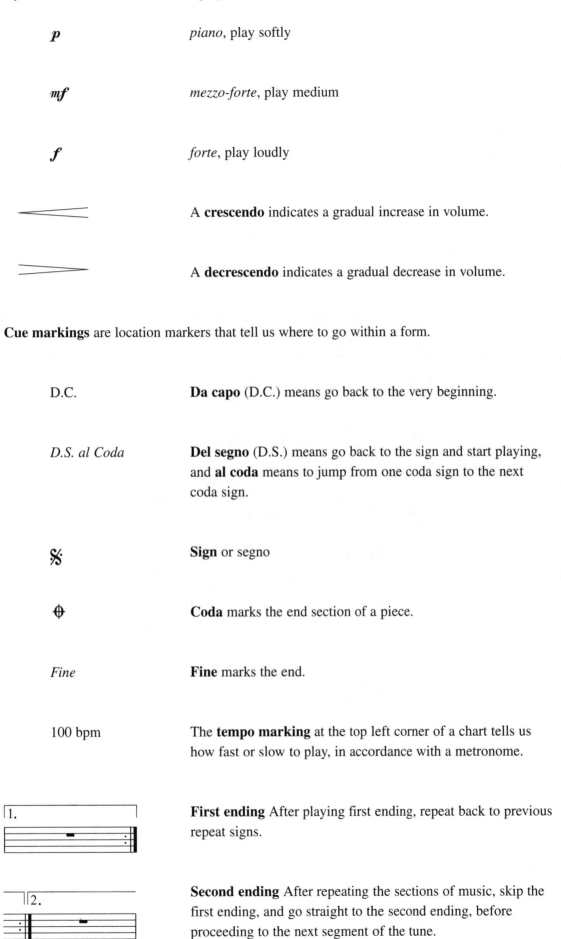	A **crescendo** indicates a gradual increase in volume.
	A **decrescendo** indicates a gradual decrease in volume.

Cue markings are location markers that tell us where to go within a form.

D.C.	**Da capo** (D.C.) means go back to the very beginning.
D.S. al Coda	**Del segno** (D.S.) means go back to the sign and start playing, and **al coda** means to jump from one coda sign to the next coda sign.
𝄋	**Sign** or segno
⊕	**Coda** marks the end section of a piece.
Fine	**Fine** marks the end.
100 bpm	The **tempo marking** at the top left corner of a chart tells us how fast or slow to play, in accordance with a metronome.
	First ending After playing first ending, repeat back to previous repeat signs.
	Second ending After repeating the sections of music, skip the first ending, and go straight to the second ending, before proceeding to the next segment of the tune.

Following a Chord Chart

Here's a basic drum chart. Follow along with the listening track. Try identifying all the parts of the chart before counting or playing.

How to Follow a Chart

> **Step 1**. Start by determining tempo and groove feel. This tune has a quarter-note tempo of 100 bpm, a Latin feel, and a 4/4 time signature.
>
> **Step 2**. At rehearsal letter A, notice the repeat sign.
>
> **Step 3**. Check out the sign at rehearsal letter A5.
>
> **Step 4**. Notice the coda sign, and the first and second ending.

When following the chart as you listen to track 49, here is how the tune proceeds:

> 1. Play the first four bars of the Intro groove.
>
> 2. Play from rehearsal letter A to the repeat.
>
> 3. Repeat back to A, and this time, continue on to B.
>
> 4. After B, play A with the repeat (2 times).
>
> 5. Continue B. At the fifth measure after B, take the coda.
>
> 6. Skip to the coda sign and play to the end.

Suelo's Tune

Intro

Drums and guitar only

Straight 8th Latin Feel

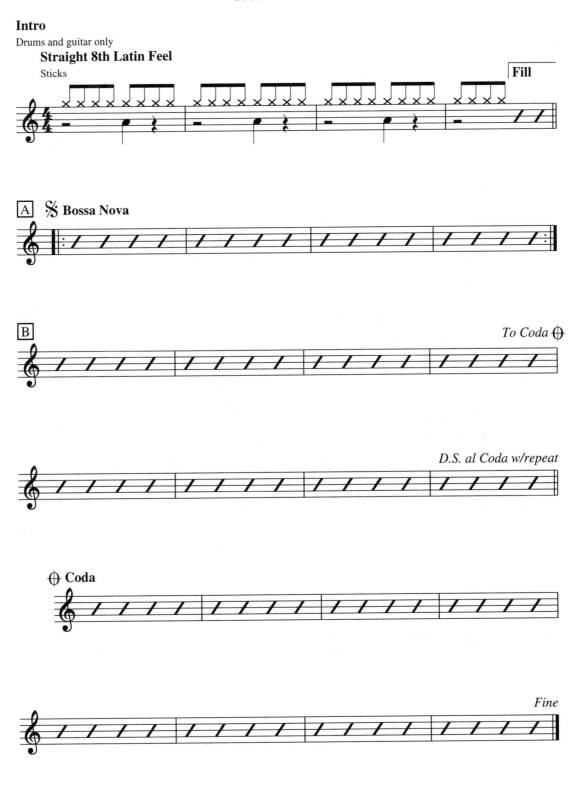

CHAPTER 8. Rudiments

Practicing rudiments will help you to play everything clearly, evenly, and consistently. Using a metronome while you practice them will help you play grooves (beats) in a steady, relaxed manner.

Practice Steps

1. Start by practicing each rudiment slowly and evenly with the metronome at 60 bpm.

2. Gradually get faster as you feel comfortable.

3. Begin experimenting with combinations of rudiments.

4. Grace notes (for flams, drags, and ratamacues) should always be played very softly. As a general rule:
   a. Start grace notes 1 inch from the drum.
   b. Start full strokes 5 inches from the drum.
   c. Start accented notes 7 inches from the drum.

Rudiments

1. Single-Stroke Roll
   Always start single strokes slowly, focusing on playing an even tone between the alternating strokes and playing with a smooth, relaxed motion.

2. Double-Stroke Roll
    Use a slight increase in fulcrum (the balance point on the stick where the thumb and index finger are placed) to control the bounce of the stick. This will help to make the second stroke of each hand equal to the first.

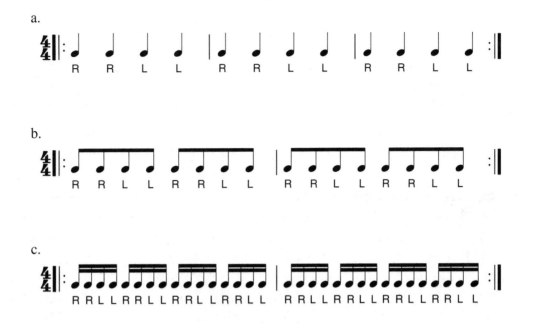

a.

R   R   L   L   R   R   L   L   R   R   L   L

b.

R   R   L   L   R   R   L   L   R   R   L   L   R   R   L   L

c.

R R L L R R L L R R L L R R L L   R R L L R R L L R R L L R R L L

PRACTICE TIP

For rudiments 3 to 9, on all short rolls (5, 7, 9, 10, 11, 13, and 15), focus on practicing even double strokes with slight squeeze on the second stroke(s).

3. 5-Stroke Roll

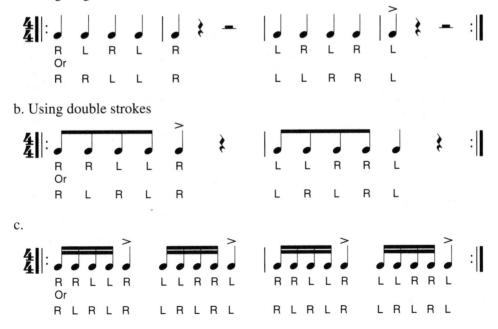

a. Using single strokes

R   L   R   L   R   L   R   L   R   L
Or
R   R   L   L   R   L   L   R   R   L

b. Using double strokes

R   R   L   L   R   L   L   R   R   L
Or
R   L   R   L   R   L   R   L   R   L

c.

R R L L R   L L R R L   R R L L R   L L R R L
Or
R L R L R   L R L R L   R L R L R   L R L R L

4. 7-Stroke Roll

a.

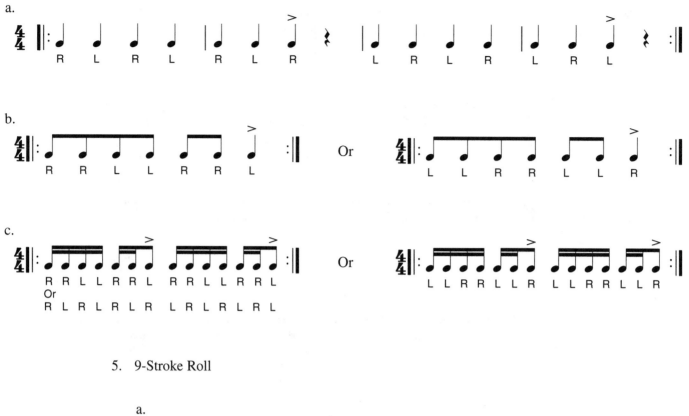

b.

Or

c.

Or

5. 9-Stroke Roll

a.

b.

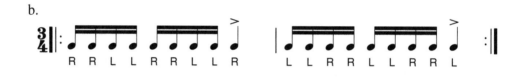

6. 10-Stroke Roll

a.

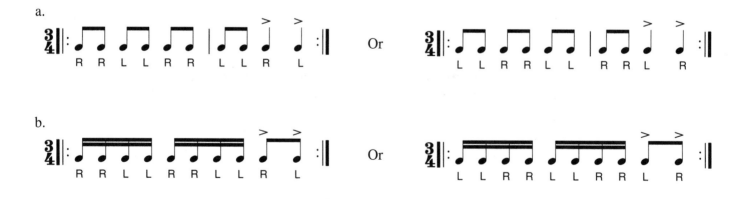

Or

b.

Or

7. 11-Stroke Roll

a.

Or

b.

Or

8. 13-Stroke Roll

a.

b.

9. 15-Stroke Roll

a.
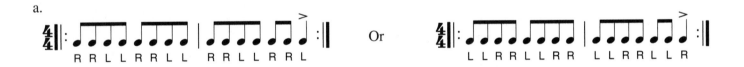

Or

b.

Or

PRACTICE TIP

For rudiments 10 and 11, on single and double paradiddles, be sure to use two different stick heights: 7 inches for the accented notes and 5 inches for the unaccented notes. Control the bounce of the double strokes with the fulcrum.

10. Single Paradiddle

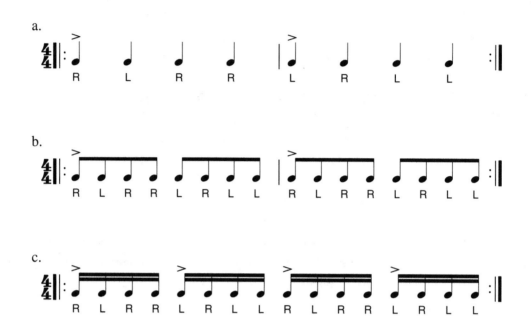

11. Double Paradiddle

PRACTICE TIP

For rudiments 12 to 16, on flams, maintain consistent separation in the distance between the hands. The grace note hand is low and strikes the drum right before the full stroke. Flam tap, flam accent, etc. all use three different stick heights.

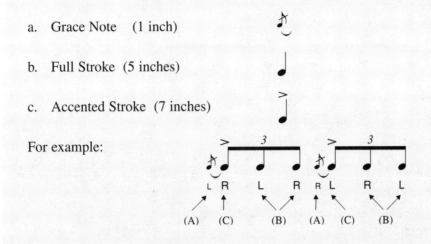

a. Grace Note   (1 inch)

b. Full Stroke (5 inches)

c. Accented Stroke (7 inches)

For example:

12. Flam

   The grace note is played just before the full stroke, softly.

   a. Right and Left Flams

   b. Alternating Flams

13. Flam Tap

   a.

   b.

   c.

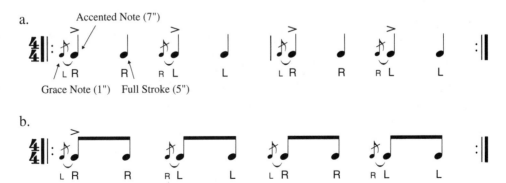

14. Flam Accent

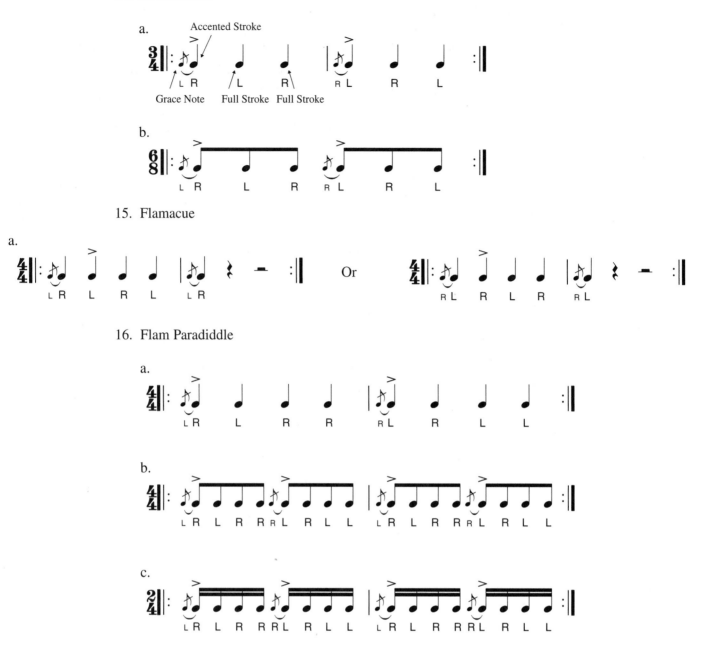

15. Flamacue

16. Flam Paradiddle

PRACTICE TIP

For rudiments 17 to 25, the ruff (rough) is one of the most difficult. The two grace notes should always be soft, and the accented notes should be 7 inches high. Use fulcrum pressure to keep the bounce stroke under control and even.

For example:

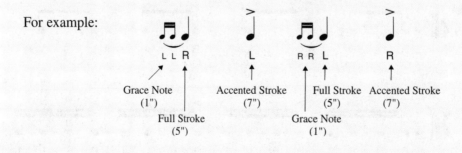

17. Half Drag (sometimes called a "ruff")
Play grace notes softly, with the stick 1 inch from the drum.

Note: As with flams, the grace notes are played very softly and the full stroke is played at medium volume. (Start 6 inches from the drum.)

19. Double Drag

a.

b.

20. Ratamacue

a.

b.

21. Double Ratamacue

22. Triple Ratamacue

23. Drag Paradiddle 1

a.

b.

c.

Conclusion

Thank you for sharing your talent with *8 Essentials of Drumming: Grooves, Fundamentals, and Musicianship*. With regular practice and some quality time "jamming" with other musicians, mastering these eight essential areas will help you on your way to a lifetime of enjoying musical performance. Though we have visited some of the essentials of making music with drums, there is always more to learn. Whenever possible, seek the advice of more experienced drummers, and always keep "open ears" and an open mind.

Keep swinging,

Ron Savage

About the Author

Ron Savage is a drummer, clinician, and educator, and has played with Art Farmer, Joe Zawinul, Albert King, Mulgrew Miller, Don Byron, and many others. He has taught thousands of drummers, and is author of *Berklee Instant Drumset* and co-author of *The Berklee Practice Method: Drums*. Ron Savage chairs the Ensemble Department at Berklee College of Music.

Create.
learn music online

Berkleemusic is the Continuing Education Division of Berklee College of Music. Study music production, guitar and bass, songwriting, music business, theory, harmony, and ear training from anywhere in the world with Berklee's renowned faculty. Over 100 online courses and certificate programs are enrolling now!

Popular Courses and Programs include:
- Music Theory 101 12-week course
- Critical Listening 12-week course
- Guitar Chords 101 12-week course
- Master Certificate in Producing 8-course program

Online Courses and Programs Enrolling Now!

Call Our Student Advisors Today
1.866.BERKLEE
berkleemusic.com

Berklee music ™
learn music online

Great New Drum Releases From Berklee Press

DRUM SET WARM-UPS
ESSENTIAL EXERCISES FOR IMPROVING TECHNIQUE
By Rod Morgenstein
Legendary drummer Rod Morgenstein reveals his innovative warm-up method designed to limber up your entire body. Features exercises to develop and improve your speed, power, control, coordination, independence, accuracy, endurance and agility.
50449465 ....$12.95

RUDIMENT GROOVES FOR DRUM SET
By Rick Considine
Rudiments are the drum language: a basic vocabulary of rhythms that drummers arrange and rearrange when they play grooves, solos and fills. This book shows you how to apply them to the drum set in all styles of music. Fifty illustrated grooves are reinforced on the accompanying CD so you can hear how the rudiments should sound when you apply them to the drum set.
50448001 ....$19.95

BASIC AFRO-CUBAN RHYTHMS FOR DRUM SET AND HAND PERCUSSION
Featuring Ricardo Monzón
Learn how to play and practice the classic rhythms of the Afro-Cuban tradition with Berklee professor Ricardo Monzón. You'll play along as he starts slowly with the basic patterns, then increases the tempo with a number of variations. By the end, you'll have a solid understanding of how to play and practice essential Afro-Cuban rhythms.
55 minutes.
50448012 ....$19.95

BERKLEE PRACTICE METHOD: DRUM SET
By Ron Savage, Casey Scheuerell and the Berklee Faculty
This sensational series lets you improve your intuitive sense of timing and improvisation, develop your technique and reading ability, and master your role in the groove. Play along with a Berklee faculty band on the accompanying CD, then play with your own band!
50449429 ....$14.95

The Reading Drummer – Second Edition
By Dave Vose
This Berklee Workshop is ideal for both beginners and pros and includes everything you'll need to make sightreading drum notation easy and natural. Features: more than 50 lessons complete with general practice tips; steady learning progression from reading quarter notes to 16th-note triplets; practice rhythms containing accents, flams, rolls, ruffs, tempo and meter changes; and much more.
50449458 ....$9.95

BEYOND THE BACKBEAT
FROM ROCK & FUNK TO JAZZ & LATIN
By Larry Finn
Learn how to take any basic rock/funk drum beat and morph it into jazz and world music feels. Improve your chops, expand your versatility, and develop your own style. The accompanying CD features over 90 play-along tracks to test out your morphing techniques as you groove with a Berklee band in all contemporary styles.
50449447 ....$19.95

FOR MORE INFORMATION, SEE YOUR LOCAL MUSIC DEALER, OR WRITE TO:

7777 W. BLUEMOUND RD. P.O. BOX 13819 MILWAUKEE, WI 53213

Also Available:
The Studio/Touring Drummer DVD/50448034 ....$19.95
Latin Jazz Grooves DVD/50448003 ....$19.95
Mastering the Art of Brushes/50449459 ....$19.95
Berklee Instant Drum Set/50449513 ....$14.95
Brazilian Rhythms/50449507 ....$29.95

Visit Hal Leonard Online at
www.halleonard.com

Visit Berklee Press Online at
www.berkleepress.com
call us at 1·800·554·0626